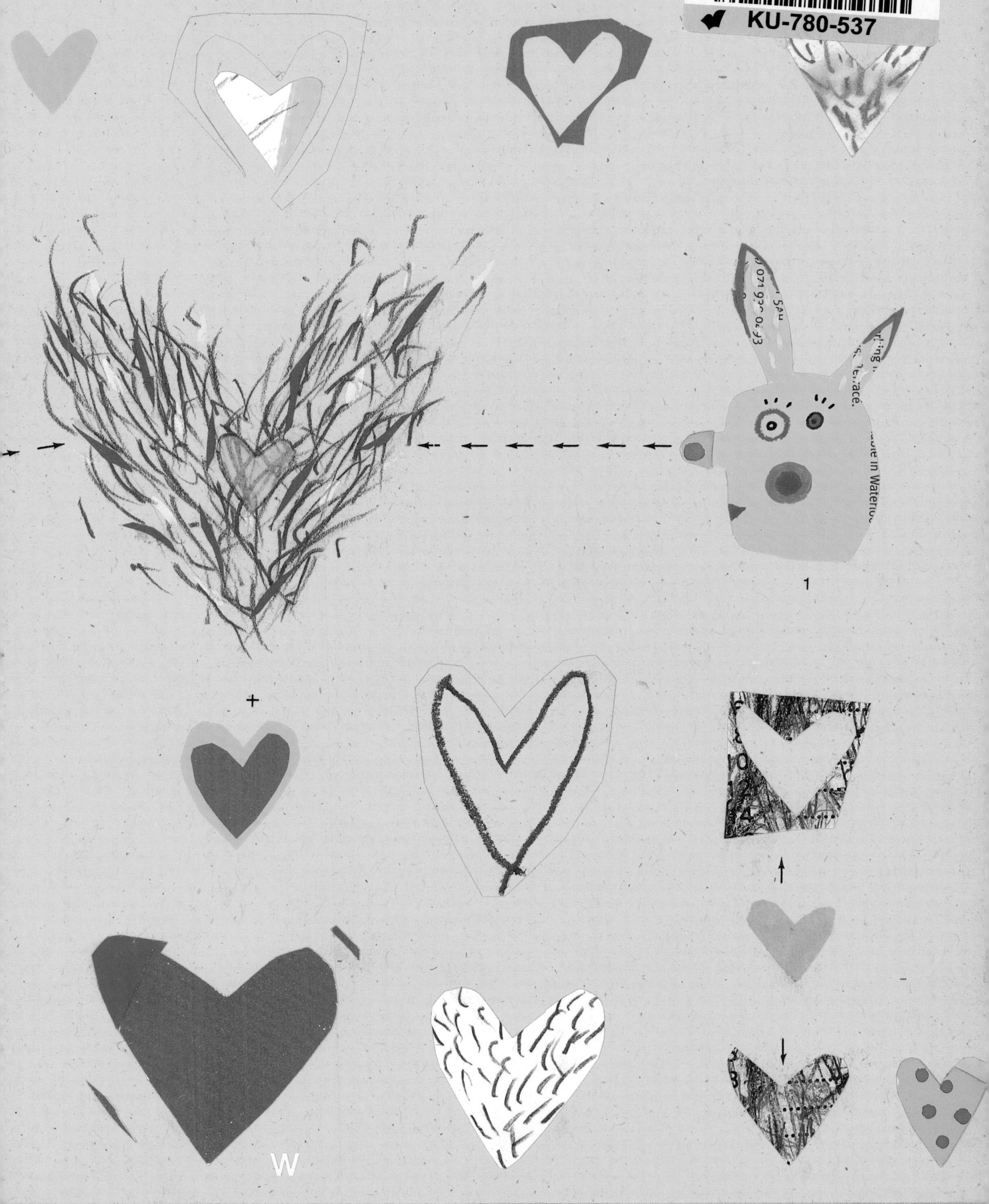

Wolf!

Sara Fanelli

Heinemann

FOR
MARIO & LINUCCIA
J.B. & EMILY
papà GION & mamma ROSALIE

5·94   8·95   1·96

First published in Great Britain 1997
by William Heinemann Limited
an imprint of Reed International Books Limited
Michelin House, 81 Fulham Road, London SW3 6RB
and Auckland, Melbourne, Singapore and Toronto

0 434 97650 4

Produced by Mandarin Offset Limited
Printed and bound in China

It was a

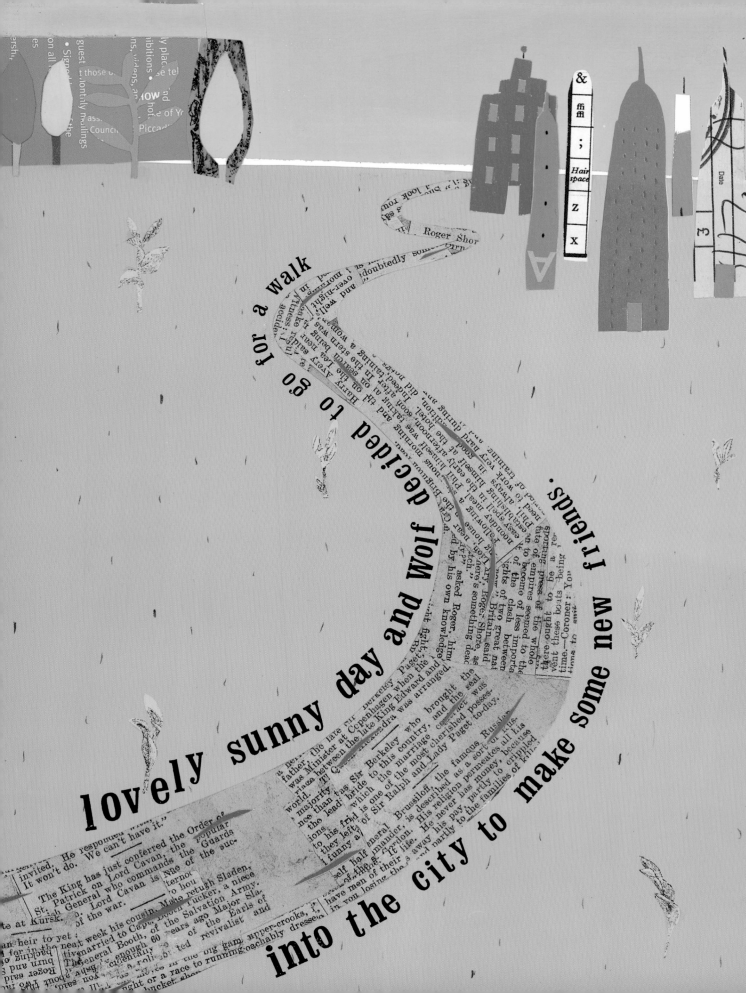

lovely sunny day and Wolf decided to go for a walk into the city to make some new friends.

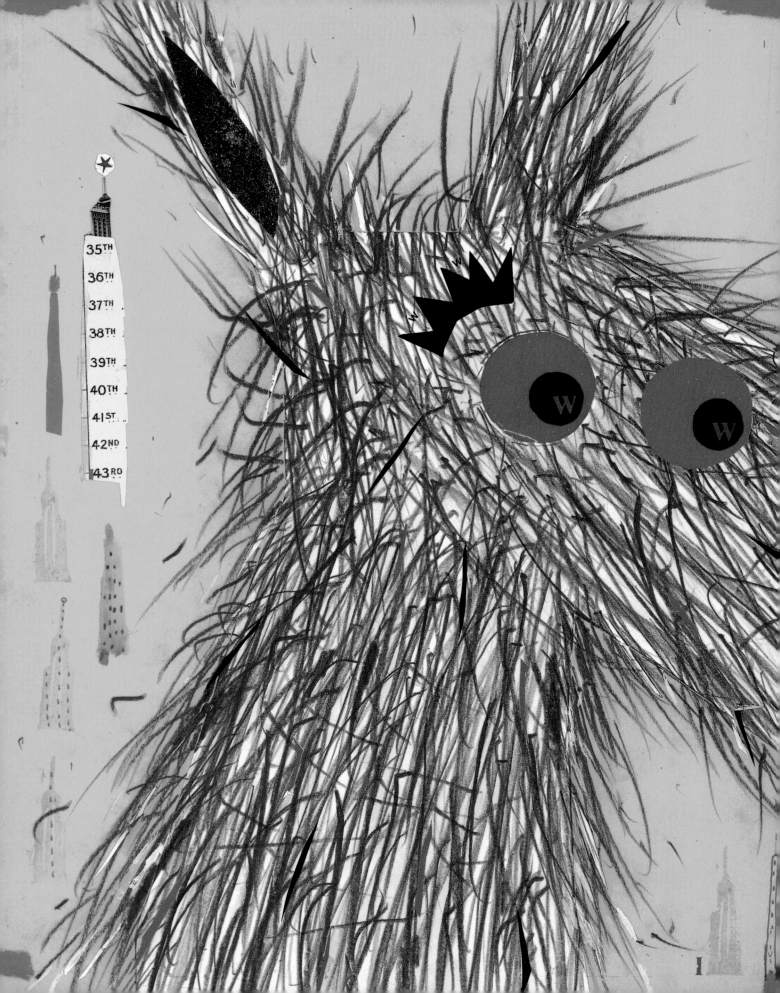

35TH
36TH
37TH
38TH
39TH
40TH
41ST
42ND
43RD

W
W
W
W

I

On the road Wolf met an old lady searching for her spectacles.

Wolf tried to be helpful
and found them for her.
But, after she had put
them back on and could
see again, she peered at
Wolf and ran away in
fright. Wolf was sorry
she had not stayed
for a chat.

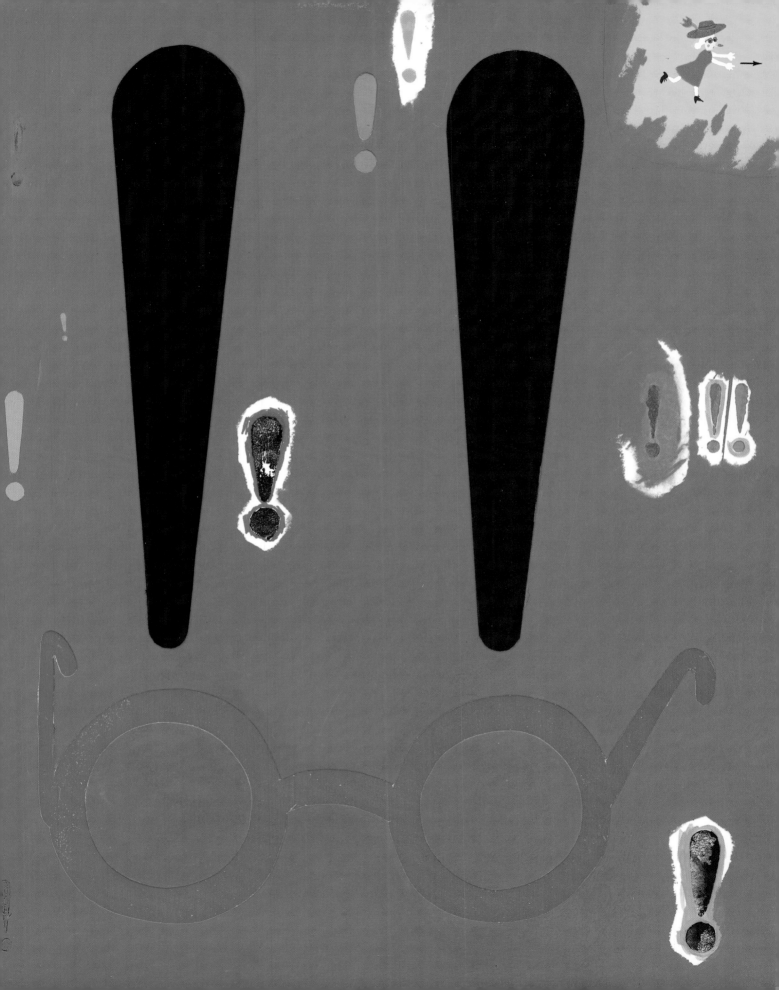

Further on, Wolf saw a **big** bright car that a man was busily repairing.

Wolf wanted to help him too and began
handing him the tools.

After the job
was finished,
the man stood
with a startled
look and

chased wolf away.

WVUT

Next Wolf came
upon a group of
children playing
with masks.
They thought
that he too was
wearing a mask
and asked him
to join the game.

Wolf was so happy and enjoyed playing with them.

But Something Went Wrong.

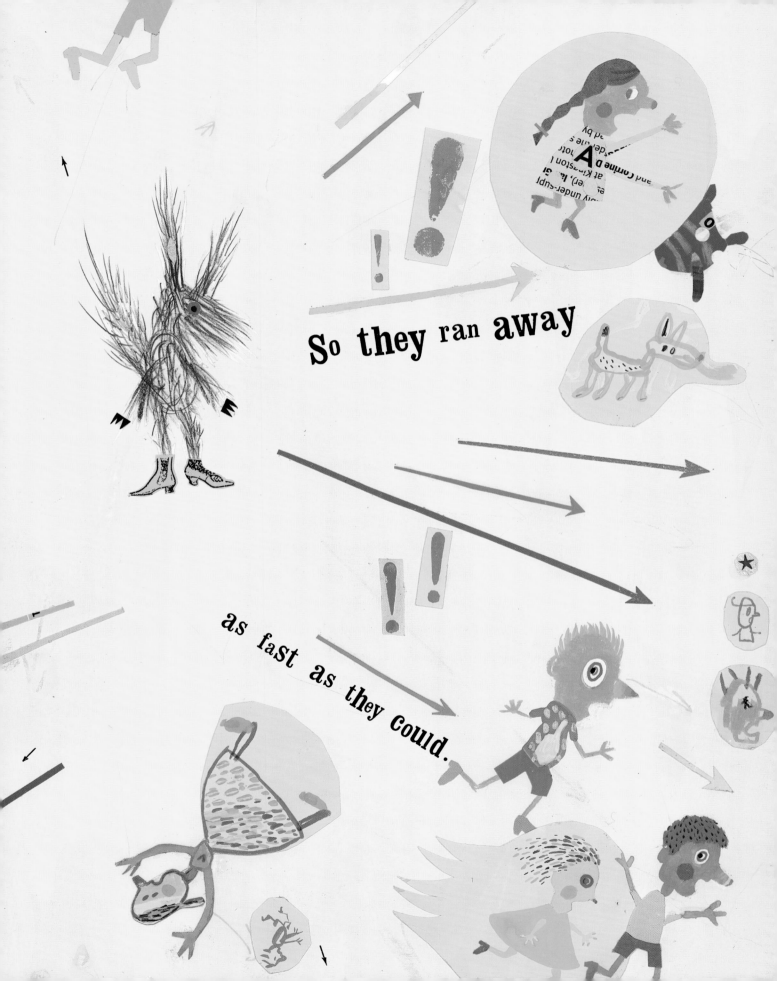

So they ran **away**

as fast as they could.

Wolf was very sad because they did not want to be his friends. However, he had an idea.

Maybe if he did wear a mask he could make some friends.

Then a barber saw him and thought Wolf needed a shave. He invited him into his shop.

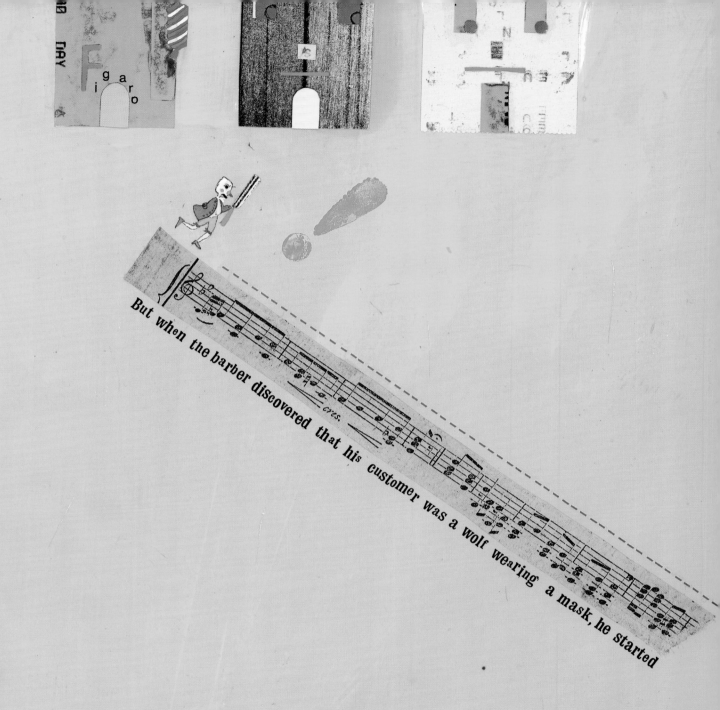

But when the barber discovered that his customer was a wolf wearing a mask, he started

chasing after Wolf with his razor!

Running fast to
escape, Wolf finally
reached a garden
where he stopped
to hide and to
catch his breath.

But very soon the gardener arrived

and started watering the plants.

And Wolf had to
start running
again.
It seemed
everyone
was after him.

Wet and alone, Wolf

felt sad. He had tried

35

to be   friendly   but   everyone   he'd

met   had found   him   fierce   and   scary.

Finally, he was

It was his friend Rosie and Wolf told her about his many misadventures and misunderstandings.

who smiled at him.

going home when he suddenly caught sight of someone

All the people
he had met in the city
were astonished to hear his words.
They suddenly realized

Vous voilà,   bien instruite sur

how wrong
they had been to think
Wolf was a ferocious creature.
Really he was very amiable !

they all had a wonderful picnic.